Life in the Spirit:
A Study on the Holy Spirit

T
TOPICAL
STUDY

Expert Press
www. ExpertPress.net

Website: dailydisciples.org

ISBN-13: 978-0692594834
ISBN-10: 0692594833

DAILY disciples
Psalm 113:3

LIFE IN THE SPIRIT

A Study on the Holy Spirit

The Holy Spirit is an equal member of the Trinity who indwells and lives within the hearts of all who have accepted Jesus Christ as Savior. But what advantage does He give to us today? Who is the Holy Spirit and what is His role today? There are a multitude of questions and misconceptions about the Holy Spirit. This study is designed to give the Christian an overview of the roles and functions of the Holy Spirit. This study will also address who He is, what He does, and how He works in our lives and through our lives. The Bible is the only source needed to find answers for the questions within the study. Regardless of denominational affiliation or religious background, this study will provide insight into the powerful workings of the Holy Spirit for the body of Christ. ***For by one Spirit we were all baptized into one body—whether Jews or Greeks, whether slaves or free—and have all been made to drink into one Spirit. (1 Corinthians 12:13)***

This 4-lesson study consists of four main topics on the Holy Spirit:

- **Believe and Receive**: How do we receive the Holy Spirit?
- **Baptism and Beyond**: How do we receive more and why do we need more of the Holy Spirit?
- **Evidence or Incidence**: What evidence should be seen of the Holy Spirit in our lives and what incidence happens when there is no evidence of Him in our lives?
- **Gifts and Callings**: What gifts does the Holy Spirit give, how are they used in us and for what purposes?

Each lesson consists of questions, commentaries and applicable scriptural readings. No outside materials are required or needed to complete this study. We ask that you pray for the Lord to open your minds before you begin any Bible reading and homework. The Holy Spirit will be your Teacher as He will lead you to understand more of His powerful and active role in your daily life.

For more information, visit us at www.dailydisciples.org or call 1-800-992-0369.

Contents

Lesson 1 Introduction:

Believe and Receive

How do we receive the Holy Spirit? What happens when we receive Him? How do we embrace the Holy Spirit and His roles in our lives? There are many questions concerning the Holy Spirit. The first week of the study will be an introduction to the Holy Spirit and what it means to live a Spirit-filled life. Our desire is to lay a scriptural foundation of who the Holy Spirit is and how He affects our daily lives. The foundation to everything, however, is Jesus. Let's begin with our relationship to Him.

The gospel of John starts by discussing Jesus, the Word, coming as the Light into the world. Those of us who receive Jesus and believe in His name become God's children. ***"But as many as received Him, to them He gave the right to become children of God, to those who believe in His name" John 1:12.*** John the Baptist was a contemporary of Jesus but John's ministry started first. He was the forerunner to prepare the way for the Messiah. He had one main point when preaching—Repent! John's ministry was to prepare the hearts of the people to realize that they were sinners who needed a Savior. John baptized with water symbolic of the need for cleansing. As Jesus appeared at the Jordan River, John knew who Jesus was. Though John considered himself unworthy, Jesus asked John to baptize Him also. During His baptism, the Holy Spirit visually descended upon Jesus "like a dove" (John 1:31-32). Jesus began His earthly ministry soon after His baptism. Jesus would not baptize with water but with fire, representing the power and authority He has to change each life He touches. That baptism continues today.

We become Christians by accepting the sacrifice that Jesus gave on the cross for our sins and knowing that we can do nothing to please God without His blood covering us. By accepting Jesus as our Savior, we receive the Holy Spirit and are sealed with the Holy Spirit for eternity (Ephesians 1:13-14). The apostle Paul would write to the church at Ephesus and tell them that for those who have believed in Jesus Christ and trusted in His redemptive works, they have also received His inheritance, guaranteed and sealed by His Holy Spirit.

We as believers become the temple of the Holy Spirit. He lives within us, never leaves us and goes everywhere we go. The Holy Spirit is boundless and limitless and has no form or substance. Jesus described Him as being like the wind. We cannot see the wind or know from where it comes, but we can see the evidence of it. Water and oil are other illustrations used to describe the Holy Spirit in scripture.

In John 4:23, Jesus tells us that true worshipers need to worship in Spirit and in truth. The Spirit is first because we have no ability to even understand the scriptures without the Holy Spirit. As believers who have received the Spirit, we must pray for our minds to be opened so that we can comprehend His word. We also must pray that we can have a balance of both Spirit and truth as we grow in our relationship with Him. If one side is out of balance, either too much Spirit or too much truth, we can miss out on what God has for us. Too much Spirit can lead to expressions and emotions that elicit good feelings but may be lacking in truthful foundations to sustain a solid walk. On the other hand, too much truth can lead to a legalistic attitude that has no spiritual flexibility. We are to be as clay in the Potter's hands, able to be shaped and changed, able to surrender to the Lord's will. We need a balance.

Finally, lesson one wraps up with what the Holy Spirit should look like in our lives. There should be some evidence of His working in us and through us. We will study this evidence more fully in lesson three of the study. But we will take a glimpse of the fruits of the Spirit as we start to think about how we live a Spirit-filled life. Our hearts' desire is to understand who we are in Christ because of the power of the Holy Spirit that lives within us to accomplish the work of God through us.

We pray that this lesson is life changing for each of us. As Christians, it is time to embrace the power within us as we are the temples of the Holy Spirit (1 Corinthians 3:16) and to start living our lives in the freedom granted to us by the mercy and grace of our Lord and Savior Jesus Christ.

Dear heavenly Father, we ask that You fill us now with Your Holy Spirit to open our minds and hearts so that we may comprehend Your word and have the power to walk in Your ways.

Please give us the desire and commitment to read and study Your word, to pray without ceasing and to apply the knowledge and wisdom given by You to live Spirit-filled lives. We pray that today is a first step to life in the Spirit. We love and praise You. In Jesus name, Amen.

Lesson 1: Believe and Receive

Read John 1, John 3, Ephesians 1

The Holy Spirit is a distinctive, divine person. He is the third person of the trinity: the Father, the Son and the Holy Spirit (Matthew 28:19). He has existed and has been present from the beginning as Genesis 1:1-2 says, *"In the beginning God created the heavens and the earth. The earth was without form and void; and darkness was on the face of the deep. And the Spirit of God was hovering over the face of the waters."* The Holy Spirit does not draw attention to Himself but without Him, we cannot understand the Bible. The word of God is written by the Spirit and is comprehended because of the Spirit. His works and presence are clearly seen and, at times, mentioned throughout the Bible. In the Old Testament scriptures, He directed, guided, counseled and instructed persons individually for the leading of the nation of Israel as a whole. The Spirit gifted the men to build the tabernacle, the Spirit filled men at times with the gift of prophecy, the Spirit anointed David to be king of Israel, and so the Spirit was continually active throughout history. Through the nation of Israel, God laid a foundation for His purposes and plans to send His Son, Jesus, into the world for the redemption of sin. The role of the Holy Spirit interacting with an individual is different between the Old Testament and the New Testament. The Holy Spirit was not fully released to seal and empower individuals until after Jesus was glorified (John 7:39). John 1 says that the Word was in the beginning (just as the Spirit) and the Word became flesh and dwelt among us. Jesus came to earth fully God and fully man and He, Himself, was filled with the Holy Spirit to accomplish the work determined by God the Father. With His ascension into heaven after His resurrection, the Holy Spirit would be released upon all who believed. Receiving begins with believing…

Part 1: We Believe

Question 1: ***Read John 1:10-13*** to answer the following questions.

a. Who is John describing in these verses?

Jesus

b. Who did He come for?

[illegible] Jesus

c. What was promised to those who believe?

to become children of God

Believe means to entrust one's spiritual well being; to have faith in Christ. Receive means to take, to get hold of. John is saying that by entrusting our spiritual well being in Christ through faith, we take hold of all Jesus did for us (restoring our relationship back to God) and then we receive all the fullness of the promises given from the beginning of creation.

Question 2: **Read John 3:1-5** to answer the following questions.

a. Where does Nicodemus say that Jesus comes from?

God

b. What evidence has Nicodemus seen to make this statement?

signs - miracles

c. What does Jesus say in reply?

Born of water & Spirit

Jesus gives further detail in verse 5. Describe what happens for us to enter the kingdom of God?

Unless they are born again

Mathew 11:11

Question 3: **From John 3:6-11,**

a. How does Jesus describe the Spirit?

By Wind

b. Who is Jesus speaking of in verse 11?

God, Jesus

Question 4: How have you personally viewed the Holy Spirit in your life? Take time to write down your comments, perceptions and questions about Him.

I know

Jesus tells us that we are physically born first of flesh but we must be born of the Spirit (or in Jesus' words, "born again"). We become born again by believing in His finished work on the cross, knowing that we cannot have a relationship with the Father without the blood of Christ making atonement for our sins. The moment we accept Jesus as our personal Savior, we receive the Holy Spirit. It is a simple prayer: ***"Dear Lord I know I am a sinner. I know that You sent Your Son to die on the cross, shedding His blood for my sins. I ask You Jesus to come into my heart and save me. I surrender control of my life to You. Please fill me with Your Holy Spirit and lead me in Your ways. Thank You for saving me."***

When Adam and Eve were created, their spirit was alive and in direct relationship with God. After their choice to disobey God's command, the consequence of their sin was two fold.

Physically, their bodies of flesh would die in time but spiritually, they died that day. As a result, we are all born spiritually dead (Romans 5:12). Jesus came to restore the relationship that was severed in the Garden. Today, our flesh will still die physically but we now have the choice to have a spiritual life with God, starting here yet lasting for eternity with God. In John 6:63, Jesus said, "*it is the Spirit who gives life; the flesh profits nothing. The words that I speak to you are spirit and they are life.*"

Part 2: We Receive

Question 5: ***Read Ephesians 1:13-14*** to answer the following questions.

a. After hearing the word of truth, what 2 things must we do?

~~trust~~ hear the word of God
seal with the holy spirit

b. What happens next?

c. What is He?

the guaronty of our
enheritage

d. What does this mean to you personally?

knowing that we have a
heavenly place

This seal of the Holy Spirit is like a stamp on the back of a letter. In ancient times, the King would place his seal on a letter, indicating that the letter was officially from him. Paul uses the same word to describe what happens to us after believing and trusting in Jesus. We receive His seal of the Holy Spirit, guaranteeing that we belong to Him. God promises us that we receive God Himself through the Spirit. The Spirit never leaves us because He has sealed us. This same term, sealed, is also used in Revelation 7:3-8 describing those who are sealed (or stamped) on their foreheads, indicating that they are servants of God.

Question 6: ***From John 14:14-17 & 26,***

a. What does Jesus promise His disciples? (see verses 14 & 16)

ask anything in
my name

b. From verses 14 & 26, what is the significance of His name?

Question 7: Look up the following verses to answer this question: What are some of the roles of the Holy Spirit in our lives?

a. John 14:26

guider, consolor,
conviction

b. John 15:26

c. John 16:13

d. Acts 9:31

e. Romans 8:26

f. 1 Corinthians 6:11

g. 1 John 2:27

The Holy Spirit has unlimited roles in that He is living and active in the world today. Only Jesus could live in a physical body and have a complete balance in the gifts and roles of the Holy Spirit. When Jesus departed from earth, He promised that the Holy Spirit would dwell in His disciples (John 14:17). As we become His disciples, we represent Jesus as He has given each of us His Holy Spirit. Paul says in 1 Corinthians 3:16 that we are the temple of the Holy Spirit as He lives in each of us. Being His temple means that where ever you are or whatever you are dealing with, so is God. Whatever you face, go through, think or feel, He knows. God is with you. Every aspect of your life, He wants to be a part of and be included in. That is why Jesus came to earth...for God to dwell with us (John 1:14). Collectively, we make up the house of God. And individually, we have roles to be accomplished in us and through us.

So, what does God desire most from us as His temples? The answer is: for God to be glorified. God wants to be glorified in everything we do. God wants us to bear much fruit so He can be glorified (John 15:8). He wants us to pray and ask for anything and everything so that He is glorified through us. In John 14:13, Jesus said "*And whatever you ask in my name, that I will do, that the Father may be glorified in the Son.*" So, we can pray about everything from grocery lists, to car pool lines to business meetings and the salvation of others, because the more we pray, the more glory the Lord receives for doing the work through us. We have all been given one Spirit by which He gifts and calls us for the body of Christ. The Spirit teaches, helps, intercedes, comforts, exhorts, trains us in every situation if we fully rely on God. As believers, we each represent a function of the body with Jesus as the head and the Holy Spirit as the One who equips us to do the work of the Lord. No task is too small and no prayer is too menial. We are God's! He rewards faith and wants the glory. Every time we pray, we act in faith. Every time He answers (even if it is no), we can give Him glory. We should be walking worshippers of the Lord Jesus, having a balance of Spirit and truth, fully equipped and empowered for every good work.

Question 8: **From John 4:23-24,**

a. How are we to worship?

In spirit and truth

b. Define these 2 ways of worship.

knowledge

c. How do we as believers apply both of these to our lives?

We need to worship in Spirit which we receive through believing in the truth of Christ. Every chapter, verse and page of the Bible tells us the truth of Christ and by this truth we are sanctified (or set apart for God). We have to believe in the complete word of God as Truth. The word of God is written by the Spirit. We need the Spirit to open our minds so that we can comprehend and understand the truth of His words. The Spirit leads, guides, instructs, exhorts and corrects us on how to live out the truth in our every day lives to please the Lord. The Spirit-filled life has a balance of worship in both Spirit and Truth and this balance enables us to live in the fulfillment of God's plans and purposes for us here on earth.

Question 9: ***How do we know we walk in the Spirit? See Galatians 5:16-26.***
If we truly worship the Father in Spirit and Truth, our words, behaviors and actions should reflect His Spirit. We are called to represent Jesus. His Spirit is characterized by these fruits being evident in our lives.

determination to
touch Jesus

dug example
- dirty
- from the pin

Rom 10:12, 11
John 3:14

Sometimes we don't
look for evidence
We need to start
expecting of Gods
Word.

Question 10: What areas of your life bear witness of Him? What areas do not?

Believe & Receive

Expect something from God everyday.

God is Spirit but Colossians 2:9 further explains that "*For in Him [Jesus] dwells all the fullness of the Godhead bodily*" (NKJV) and "*All the fullness of the Deity lives in bodily form.*" (NIV) If we have come to know Jesus, we will come to have a relationship with the Father for John 14:9 says, "…*He who has seen Me, has seen the Father*…" We also become born again, receiving the Spirit of God. Everyone who has accepted Jesus Christ as their Lord and Savior, believing in His finished work on the cross and covered by His blood for the remission of sins, has received Him. By receiving Jesus, one also receives the Holy Spirit of promise, who is our guarantee of the inheritance in heaven because we were chosen before the foundation of the world.

We believe then we receive. If you have accepted Jesus as your Savior and have been born again, then you have the Holy Spirit living within you. But, what does that mean to us realistically and personally? How do we live in the power of His presence? How do we have a full life in the Spirit? The next section of the study addresses these questions and more.

Let God spoil you

"Evidence of the Spirit"

Joy & Peace

Lesson 2 Introduction:

Baptism and Beyond

As we begin the second lesson of our study on the Holy Spirit and how to live a Spirit-filled life, let's take a moment and briefly review last week's main concepts. The Holy Spirit has existed since the beginning. He is the Spirit of the trinity as there is Father, Son and Holy Spirit. Even though we learn of His presence in the Old Testament, the Spirit was not released fully until after Jesus was resurrected and ascended into heaven. For us today, to receive the Holy Spirit we must first believe in the redeeming work of Jesus Christ and in faith, believe that Jesus is the risen Son of God. Once we have accepted Christ as Savior, we are immediately filled with His Holy Spirit and our bodies become His temple here on earth. We are guaranteed as partakers of the divine inheritance and sealed for eternity. These statements are facts and promises given to us in the scriptures, but the story does not start and stop here.

In this lesson, we will examine what the Bible tells us about the baptism of the Holy Spirit. What is it? When does it happen? Why does it matter to us today? We will also discuss other concepts and terms closely identified with the baptism of the Holy Spirit such as what it means to be filled or to be continually filled, to be anointed, and whether or not we should pray for these "things." These types of questions leads us back to our main topic of this study: What does it mean to live a Spirit-filled life?

For us today, we need to learn how to apply God's word to our lives so that we are empowered as Christians. If the Bible clearly tells us that we are the temple of the Holy Spirit, that God Himself lives in each of us through His Spirit, then we need to know how to live like we believe it. Paul says in 1 Corinthians 4:20 that "*the kingdom of God is not in word but in power.*" The only way we can live a Spirit-filled life is through the power of the Holy Spirit.

We first need to know God's word. We need to be in His word daily as we pray for wisdom and understanding in knowing how to apply it. Then, through dependency on God, we are able to apply His word in power.

The Holy Spirit has many roles. Some roles we have already examined and others will examine more closely in the next two lessons. We must understand that His main purpose in us is to gift and equip us for the edification (building up) of the body of Christ. But how does all of this apply to us today?

The controversies, debates, and contradictions on this topic are countless. Just as the Spirit Himself is like the wind (not able to track Him down physically), so are the theological debates over the concepts of spiritual baptism, filling and anointing. Our goal is not to discuss debates; our goal is to teach application of God's word. For the purposes of this week's study, we will examine the original baptism of the Spirit that took place at Pentecost, the activities of the Holy Spirit in the New Testament, and how we can apply certain principles to our lives today. Before we get started, let's pray.

Dear Lord, we pray that You will lead us by Your Holy Spirit to learn how to live a Spirit-filled life. We ask that You open our minds to comprehend and understand what Your word teaches and please help us apply Your teachings to our lives today. Help us to stay focused and committed to the study of Your word and teach us how to pray for the empowering release of Your Holy Spirit within us. May we truly be an integral part of Your body, working together for the furtherance of Your kingdom. In Jesus name, Amen.

Lesson 2: Baptism and Beyond

Read Acts Chapters 2, 8, 10

In Luke 24:49 Jesus told His disciples "*Behold, I send the Promise of My Father upon you; but tarry in the city of Jerusalem until you are endued with power from on high.*" This power from on high was the promise of receiving the Holy Spirit. The promise was given many years before in the book of Joel chapter 2:28-29, "*And it shall come to pass afterward That I will pour out My Spirit on all flesh; Your sons and your daughters shall prophesy, Your old men shall dream dreams, Your young men shall see visions. And also on My menservants and on My maidservants I will pour out My Spirit in those days.*" This promise is now received because Jesus has been glorified (John 7:39), allowing us to have a relationship with the Father. As believers today, we are endued with power from on high as the Holy Spirit lives within us. But do we live in the power? The key for us is to learn what this power is and how to live in the power of His baptism.

Question 1: **Read Acts 1:4-8** to answer the following questions.

a. What did Jesus tell the disciples in verse 5?

You will baptize with the Holly Spirit

b. What were they going to receive in verse 8?

Power

c. Why was this necessary for them?

Equip us

d. How does this event apply to us today?

The two primary reasons the Holy Spirit is given with power is for the testimony and for service in Christ. On numerous occasions, the early church received an anointing of power to share the gospel of Christ through their testimony as well as to do the work of the ministry. Today, God anoints for the same purposes: sharing and service.

Question 2: **From Acts 2:1-4**, describe the sequence of events that took place.

We filled with Holly Spirit, they spoke in tongues.

The disciples were filled with the Holy Spirit as they waited in Jerusalem, just as Jesus had instructed them. The Day of Pentecost was the day in which these faithful followers were endued with the power. The evidence of the Holy Spirit was manifested through the amazing utterances of foreign tongues as witnessed by all who were present. Such a display of supernatural manifestations led many to suspect that some were drunk with wine. But Peter explained all the things that had been foretold and how it had come to pass through Jesus.

Now, the skeptics must make a decision to either accept their testimony as true and to join them or turn away in disgust and disbelief.

Question 3: **From Acts 2:37-41**, what did Peter instruct the people to do to receive the Holy Spirit?

Repent.
Change the way you think

We learned last week that the Bible teaches that we will receive the Holy Spirit when we repent from our sins and ask Jesus to forgive and save us. However, there is a lot of controversy over the terms "baptizing" or "anointing" of the Holy Spirit. Some denominations teach about the Holy Spirit from a charismatic approach while some teach from a more conservative position. During His ministry, Jesus did not always follow a predictable pattern. There was a similarity to His healing touch and teaching but not a format. The ministry of the Holy Spirit is the same.

The Spirit cannot be predicted as to where He will go or what He will do. Much controversy surrounds the teachings of the Holy Spirit because of His very own nature. No church or person should ever assume they fully understand the ways and works of God (Isaiah 55:8-9).

Question 4: What background or teachings influenced or shaped your beliefs regarding the Holy Spirit and His presence in your life?

Question 5: ***From Acts 8:14-17***, answer the following questions.

a. What did the apostles hear about Samaria?

that the acepted the gospel

b. What were the people of Samaria lacking?

c. What did Peter and John do?

they receive the Holly Spirit

d. What did the Samarians receive?

The movement of the Spirit in these verses poses further questions about the anointing of filling of the Holy Spirit. The people of Samaria had received the Word of God and had been baptized in the name of the Lord Jesus, but had not yet received the Holy Spirit. In Acts 8:16, the Scriptures say, "For as yet He [the Holy Spirit] had fallen upon none of them. They had only been baptized in the name of the Lord Jesus." Verse 17 implies that there was a visible sign associated with the believing Samaritans receiving the Holy Spirit. The Samaritans were the first people to receive salvation who were not fully Jewish. There are times when the Lord wants to confirm His gift of salvation by uniting the body of believers through the laying on of hands, prayer and visible signs.

Question 6: Read Acts 10 to answer the following questions.

a. What did Peter say at the start of his sermon in verses 34-35?

No favore

b. When did the Holy Spirit fall on those listening?

c. Why did the Jews react this way?

They were surprise
they were sircunstore

d. How did they know that God granted salvation to them?

the H

e. What happened next?

they got batize in the
Holly Spirit.

The Holy Spirit was moving upon all kinds of people as the disciples began to preach repentance and salvation through Jesus Christ. In Acts 10, the Gentiles received the Holy Spirit before water baptism, which again demonstrates the diversity of the Spirit's activities. The gift of tongues was the visible sign that God did not withhold His anointing from these Gentiles. In the book of Acts, this visible sign was very important for the establishment of the early church as it gave the apostles a clear sign of those who received salvation. This gift brought unity between the Jews and the Gentiles, thus, opening the doors for the gospel to be preached in all nations to all people. Romans 1:16 says, "*For I am not ashamed of the gospel of Christ, for it is the power of God to salvation for everyone who believes, for the Jew first and also for the Greek.*" The Greeks were Gentiles (note: a Gentile is anyone who is not Jewish). In Acts 13:2-4, the apostle Paul takes this message to the Gentiles, as he is empowered by the Holy Spirit to teach, preach and train up others to be sent out.

The book of Acts gives us a glimpse of the character of the Holy Spirit. A couple of traits stand out: He is active and He is unpredictable as each event is different and unique to the individuals involved. Later, in Acts 19 Paul spoke with a group of Ephesian believers who also believed in Jesus Christ and had been baptized with water but had not received the Holy Spirit. Just like Peter and John, Paul laid hands on them and they received the Holy Spirit.

These events not only support a visible sign of receiving the Holy Spirit but also support evidence of a separate filling or reception of Him. There was something different from the initial receiving of Him after being born again in Jesus Christ. And this topic in itself is one of theological debate and controversy. Some believe that once saved, the Holy Spirit indwells us, and that we are baptized, filled and empowered completely with the Holy Spirit. No further steps or visible signs are needed. Others believe that unless there is a visible sign, like the gift of tongues, a believer has not received the baptism of the Holy Spirit. Regardless of church doctrine and opinions, the Holy Spirit makes His dwelling place clear by the evidence of a changed life, one being conformed into the image Jesus Christ.

But what about the power of the indwelling Spirit? Do you ever wonder why you personally do not sense the power of God or His presence, even though He lives within you? Are you struggling with worldly issues but not sure how to overcome? Do you desire a Spirit filled life being poured out with His fruits, gifts and works? If the answer is "yes," then ask for more of the Holy Spirit. We need to sense His presence in a more personal way, so we need to ask for a further filling and anointing. We want more of His power everyday; therefore, we pray that we will decrease so He can increase (to have more of Him, less of us). Through prayer, we ask that the Holy Spirit will fill us, anoint us, and empower us through His gifts to be His witnesses and to serve the body of Christ. Even though we know we are the temple of the Holy Spirit, we can choose whether or not to live a life empowered by Him. But our first step begins with prayer.

Question 7: ***From Luke 11:9-13,*** Jesus gave His disciples a model prayer and instructed them to be persistent in prayer. Answer the following questions.

a. What 3 things did Jesus say to do?

Seek

b. What did Jesus promise in response?

Seek find & door will be open

c. What does Jesus tell us to ask for in verse 13?

good gifts

d. How can you apply these verses to your life today?

Today, we must also be empowered by the Holy Spirit to be an effective witness and to be active in service for Jesus Christ. We need to choose more of the Holy Spirit instead of the world. Only through His power and presence can we live a Spirit-filled life but the choice needs to be made by us every day. So often we choose to fill our hearts and minds with other things.

Question 8: Look up the following verses and describe the things that "fill" us.

a. Acts 5:17

jelousy, confusion

b. Acts 13:45

c. Acts 19:29

d. Romans 1:29

e. Ephesians 5:18

Question 9: Because we have the Holy Spirit, we are "filled" with what things of God?

a. Romans 15:14

knowledge

b. 2 Corinthians 7:4

joy, comfort

c. Ephesians 3:19

Love

d. Philippians 1:11

Richness

e. Colossians 1:9

Wisdom, understanding

f. 2 Timothy 1:4

joy

Jesus tells us to ask, seek and knock and to continue to do so without giving up. We are to be persistent and persevering in our prayers. We learn how to pray God's will through His word. We learn that He must increase and we must decrease so that His Spirit can have power and authority over us, in us and through us. The "how to" begins with each of us and the choices we make as to who is really in charge. Who sits on the throne of your life? You or God? If you sincerely desire to live a Spirit-filled life, then you must sincerely pray that you will step down and let the Lord be your Lord. You must submit and surrender your choices, the desires of your flesh, over to Him. You have all of the Holy Spirit that you will ever have, right now, today, but is He empowered to have authority in your life?

Luke 11

Ask
Seek
Knock

We need to continue to ask. in each area of your life.

Question 10: In what areas of your life today do you need the power of the Holy Spirit to be manifested? Try to list the specific areas and the problems that result.

Spiritual warfare

As believers, we are each baptized and filled with the Holy Spirit. Jesus promised Him to us and the moment we accepted to trust in Jesus Christ as Savior, we receive His Spirit. Jesus is ***the way, the truth and the life; no one comes to the Father except through Him.*** (John 14:6) Jesus left us His Holy Spirit so that we may have a personal and intimate relationship with God, the Father. We are sealed for eternity as His stamp is literally upon us. Nothing can separate us from the love of Christ (Romans 8:31-32) or from His divine inheritance (2 Peter 1:4). These promises are true, our debt has been paid and our eternity with God is sealed by His Holy Spirit. But, how do we live here on earth? How do we have heaven on earth and see the evidence of Him through our lives? To live a life filled with the Spirit means that we choose to live differently than the world. Our flesh will fight against us every step of the way and will attempt to reduce His power to a minimum in our lives, unless we exercise the power and authority within us. Our only means to do this is in planting God's word in our hearts and minds and keeping a fervent prayer life of communication with the Father.

Over the next two weeks, we will examine the evidence of the workings of Holy Spirit. Once He is empowered and in charge, then we will see changes in our lives through His fruits and His gifts.

John 14:13
John 15

Lesson 3 Introduction:

Evidence or Incidence

As we begin our third lesson of study on the Holy Spirit, let's briefly review what we have learned over the past two weeks. We must first ***believe*** in Jesus Christ and be born again. By repenting of our sins and asking Jesus to save us, we are spiritually born again. At that moment, we ***receive*** His Holy Spirit, meaning that as believers, we each have the Holy Spirit living within us.

The Holy Spirit has many prominent roles from Comforter to Teacher. He is known as "God with us" meaning that He dwells within us, comes upon us and works through us. He is also the One who opens our minds so that we can understand the teachings of the Bible and through Him we learn how to live out the truths from the Bible. The Holy Spirit grants us access to the power and presence of the Lord in our daily lives. But, understanding the works of the Holy Spirit are widely debated and have generated much controversy throughout history. He is compared to the wind, to oil and to water. All three of these move freely and are not pinned down easily.

Last week, we also discussed the topics of baptism, filling or anointing, and the need to ask for ***more*** of Him (Luke 11:13). If we need to sense His presence more personally, then we pray and ask for it. If we need to see His power working in our lives, then we pray and ask for more of His power. If we are being filled with the things of the world more than the things of the Spirit, then we ask for His help to change our habits. Life in the Spirit means living our lives in an active relationship with the Lord through the power of His Holy Spirit, reflecting His fruits and continuing to change your life from glory to glory (or to be conformed more like Jesus). Keep asking, seeking and knocking to know Him more.

In this lesson, we will discuss how the Holy Spirit is evidenced in our lives. How do we visibly see His presence and power within us? We cannot physically see the wind but we can see evidence of the wind as trees are blown and sounds are made because of its forces. The same is true of the Holy Spirit. We cannot see Him physically but we should be able to see evidence of His works. Our desire should be to see this evidence everyday but so often we just see glimpses or incidences of Him. Jesus says that we should be as a tree that bears good fruit. The tree will need to experience seasons of cold frost and painful pruning but the goal is to bear fruit. Living a life empowered by the Spirit means that we will experience similar seasons with the same goals and purposes in mind. Fruits of the Spirit include love, joy, peace, patience, kindness, goodness, faithfulness, gentleness and self-control. Are these fruits evident in your life or do they appear as incidents?

We will address the ways we can live in the fullness of the Spirit and see His evidence continually. We will also look at why we do not live in His fullness. We will discuss the difference between grieving and quenching the Holy Spirit. Both of these terms are used in the Bible in the context of disallowing the Spirit to have control. Once again, we have a choice. We can choose to yield to His will and surrender to His guidance or we can choose to harden our hearts, continue on our own path and stop His work in our lives.

If our heart's desire is to live a Spirit-filled life, then we must learn to identify the causes that keep us from fully experiencing all that God has for us. God desires for all of us to have an abundant life (John 10:10), bearing witness of knowing Jesus, evidenced by bearing the fruits of the Spirit. If we have no fruits of the Spirit, then we must examine the areas of our life that are prohibiting His active will. Before we begin this week's study, let's pray:

Dear Lord, as we begin this week of study, we pray for Your Holy Spirit to open our minds to understand Your message to each of us. We pray for soft hearts, willing and yielded to Your desires for us. We ask that You reveal to us those areas of our lives where we are grieving or quenching the work of Your Spirit. Teach us how to live a Spirit-filled life, one that bears much good fruit just like a tree, rooted and grounded in You. We praise You for Your love, grace and mercy. In Jesus name, Amen.

Lesson 3: Evidence or Incidence

Read John 15, Galatians 5, Hebrews 12

This week we are going to examine the evidence of the Holy Spirit working within our lives. The word evidence is used six times in the Bible, five in the Old Testament and once in the New Testament. The prophet Jeremiah used the word "evidence" as a form of writing like a scroll, documenting proof of something being recorded. Hebrews 11:1 uses "evidence" as something that proves or tests our faith. In essence, evidence is proof that something exists. So, as Christians there should be proof that the Holy Spirit lives within each of us. This proof or evidence is manifested through the conduct of our lives, not just sporadically but consistently. We see more incidences of the Holy Spirit in the lives of people in the Old Testament but because of Jesus, we see evidence in our Spirit filled lives today. As believers, today, we have promises that we can never lose Him, as He does not come and go. He remains and abides with us forever.

Question 1: Believers are under a different dispensation in the New Testament in comparison to the Old Testament. From the following verses, describe the behavior of the Holy Spirit in the lives of these Old Testament men.

a. Judges 16:19-20

b. 1 Samuel 16:14

c. 1 Samuel 18:12

d. Psalm 51:11

The Spirit did not dwell with man during the times of the Old Testament. The Holy Spirit would come on people, be with them, and then could depart from them. However, the prophets foretold of the coming day when the Spirit would be poured out on men and women (Joel 2:28) and would be placed within them (Ezekiel 36:26-27). The fulfillment of this prophecy would come through Jesus Christ. Luke 1 describes the Holy Spirit's activities with the parents of John the Baptist as well as with the mother of Jesus. The Holy Spirit filled the womb of John's mother, Elizabeth, before John was born. John would be the one to prepare the way for the Messiah. Later in Luke 7:28, we are told that even though there was no greater prophet born to a woman than John, he who is least in the kingdom would be greater than him. We are greater than John the Baptist because we have the Holy Spirit working in us. Because Jesus came and rose again, He left us His Holy Spirit and we receive Him here on earth, not needing to wait until heaven. Today, He makes His home within us.

Question 2: What do the following verses say about the Holy Spirit in us?

a. John 14:15-17

b. John 14:23

c. John 16:7

God promises and guarantees that we are His. The Spirit of God dwelling within us is like receiving an engagement ring from God. God gave us a promise that we will one day be united with Him and married to Him forever. 2 Corinthians 1:22 says that He has sealed us and given us His Spirit in our hearts as a guarantee. The result of this Promise should be seen as evidence of His Spirit in our lives. Our lives should bear witness to His presence and power living within us. You should sense God's prompting to speak, convicting when wrong, leading to go, changing to be more like Him, answering your prayers, exhorting to promote more faith, encouraging other believers… When you truly love the Lord and seek His presence in your daily life, you will sense His presence in all of your activities.

Question 3: What evidence is seen in your life that bears witness to the presence of the Holy Spirit working within you?

The question posed above may not be an easy one to answer. But as Christians, born again by the blood of Jesus and filled with His Spirit, we should have evidence of His presence in our lives. What should this evidence look like? Just as Jesus said that a tree is known by its fruit, so are we known by our fruit. One of the ways to examine the evidence of the Holy Spirit is to examine the fruit of the Holy Spirit within our own lives.

"For a good tree does not bear bad fruit, nor does a bad tree bear good fruit. For every tree is known by its own fruit. For men do not gather figs from thorns, nor do they gather grapes from a bramble bush."
Luke 6:43-44

Question 4: ***Read Galatians 5:1-26*** to answer the following questions.

a. From verse 16: "Walk in the _______ and you shall not fulfill the desires of the ________."

b. List the works of the flesh.

c. List the fruits of the Spirit.

d. Which do you have more of in your life?

Question 5: Rank the fruits of the Spirit in order from most to least as evidenced in your personal life.

a.

b.

c.

d.

e.

f.

g.

h.

i.

*Question 6: **The goal of the Christian life is to "bear much fruit" (John 15:5-8)***. Write a personal prayer asking the Lord to help you in the weakest areas of your fruits.

We each struggle with fruit production. For some, self-control is the hardest; for others, patience is the greatest challenge. Regardless of our weaknesses, all Jesus asked is that we are willing to confess our struggles and allow Him to work within us as He wills. Fruit is not produced naturally. It is the work of God as the believer yields to His work in their lives. The trouble we have as Christians is not being able to distinguish God's work from the circumstances. For example, many times God uses difficult people, unpleasant circumstances and challenges of life events to change us. Many Christians refuse to see these terribly difficult events as the hand of God placing limits and boundaries on their flesh to bear the fruits of the Spirit. Instead, we become frustrated, angry, overwhelmed and doubt that God is with us at all. We focus on the people and events instead of submitting to the Lord through them. It is critically important to submit to the Lord, trust in Him and to not kick against His purposes. If someone is asking you to do something against God's word or restricts you from doing what God has commanded, then you obey God, not man. But for the most part, God uses all things (including man and circumstances). The tighter the squeeze on your flesh, the greater you will see what pops out of your mouth from your heart. Fruit bearing happens when we submit in trusting the Lord for every detail of our life, like praying, "Lord, what do you have for me in this?" Instead, we tend to pray, "Why, God, why?" or "When, God, when?" However, we develop fruit by praying, "How God how? How can I be pleasing to You in this? How can I bear fruit? How can I love You better? How can I bring You glory?" For many of us, we will pray for a particular fruit but are not willing to be changed so that the fruit may begin to grow. Why is this so hard for us?

Because for fruit to grow, changes must take place. Jesus uses the fruit tree, or the vine, as a wonderfully descriptive analogy to help us better understand what must take place first.

Question 7: ***Read John 15:1-8*** to answer the following questions.

a. Jesus is the "true_________"; the Father is the _______________

b. What part of the vine do we represent?

c. What must happen before fruit is borne? (vs 4-5)

d. "If you ______ in Me, and My ______ abide in you, you will ______ what you desire, and it shall ______ for you."

e. Give 2 reasons from verse 8 for why we should bear much fruit.

1.

2.

f. What patterns or cycles of circumstances prevent you from bearing fruit?

From John 15:2, Jesus speaks of the Father needing to "prune" the branches so that they may bear more fruit. The word prune literally means to purge, to remove the unclean and the filthy. Gardeners and those who work with fruit trees know that the act of pruning is essential for the health and productivity of the tree itself. Have you ever seen a tree pruned to the point that it looks barren or naked? It is almost painful to look at something cut back to its trunk, but it is a wise gardener who knows how to skillfully yet lovingly make the cuts necessary for a fruitful season. The Lord will do the same type of pruning, or purging, in our lives. He wants to remove the unclean, the dirty and the dead parts, because He knows that those things must be removed first before we can truly begin to grow. The main difference between the fruit tree and us is that we have freedom of choice. We can choose to remain fruitless because we do not want the pain of pruning. Or, we can surrender to the Master vinedresser and let Him have His way with His pruning shears. Though painful for a season, the end results are evidenced in a fruitful life.

Question 8: What are we doing to the Holy Spirit when we refuse to allow the Lord to have His way in our lives?

a. Ephesians 4:30

b. 1 Thessalonians 5:19

c. How have you grieved or quenched the Holy Spirit in your life? Give an example.

We all are guilty of grieving and quenching the Holy Spirit's work in our lives, at least to some degree. The question is: Are we willing to let go and let Him be in control? To grieve the Holy Spirit means that we distress Him, causing Him grief and sorrow. We do this by turning to the ways of our flesh and fulfilling those desires instead of the desires of the Spirit. Many times this behavior happens because our flesh does not want to believe that God wants us uncomfortable. We fight against submitting to God and trusting that He knows and sees all that affect us. This behavior prevents the Holy Spirit from working within us and will ultimately result in fruitless efforts. It is God's will for you to have a little more love, joy, peace, patience, kindness…through whatever comes across your path. That is living the victorious Christian life. It's not about the people or circumstances changing, it is about you changing despite the people and the circumstances to reflect more of God's character. To quench the Holy Spirit means that we extinguish His work as if putting out a fire, like throwing cold water on it. The fire within us goes out, no light, and therefore, there is no evidence of Him. The apostle Paul warns us to **not** grieve or quench the Holy Spirit, due to the consequences that will come as a result. If you truly want to live for the Lord and be used by the Lord, you will welcome God's work in your life.

Question 9: ***How does the Lord treat His children when correction is necessary? Why? (See Hebrews 12:1-5).***

Question 10: How have you been challenged by this week's study? Explain.

The Holy Spirit lives within each heart of the Christian. Jesus promised that the Father would send Him to abide with us forever. Unlike in the Old Testament, He does not come and go; He will never leave us. (Hebrews 13:5) As true followers of Christ, we should bear witness of His presence in our lives and just as a good tree produces good fruit, so should we. The flesh, our human nature, wars constantly against the Spirit but it is He who convicts us of sin and teaches the truth. One of the Holy Spirit's purposes is to conform us into the image of Christ and this can only be done through a submission of our will and choices unto Him. Through a process of pruning and chastisement, our lives begin to reflect His work within us. Though painful for a moment, "afterward it yields the peaceable fruit of righteousness to those who have been trained by it." (Hebrews 12:11) We must realize that the only evidence we have to bear witness to our Savior Jesus Christ is seen in the lives we lead through the fruit we bear. John the Baptist warned the people to "bear fruits worthy of repentance" (Matthew 3:8) or else the tree would be cut off at its roots and cast into the fire. No matter what we must go through in life's trials and tribulations, every part of it should bear witness to the power and presence of the Holy Spirit living within our hearts.

Dear Lord God, I am willing to let You have Your way in my life. I give my rights over to You as I want to bear good fruit. Open my eyes so that I may be active in praying for the things You desire to change in me. I am sorry for quenching Your Spirit and for resisting Your works in me. Have Your way, Lord Jesus...in whom I pray. Amen

Lesson 4 Introduction:

Gifts and Callings

In the fourth and final lesson of our study on the Holy Spirit, we are going to examine and discuss the topic of *spiritual gifts*. Thus far we have studied who the Holy Spirit is, how we receive Him, what does His baptism mean, why we need to ask for His continual filling, and where His evidence should be seen in our lives. (Though several of these characteristics of the Holy Spirit have been discussed, further personal study of the scriptures is highly recommended. This study is not meant to be all inclusive of His character or workings.) Now, we will focus on His workings within us. Just as we looked at the evidence of Him through His fruits (love, joy, peace, patience…self-control), we need to go the next step to better understand how His work is carried out through our lives that are surrendered to His control.

The topic of spiritual gifts is exciting for Christians and most of us are eager to learn more. Before we dig into the specific gifts and purposes they serve, we must understand the basics. Spiritual gifts are not given for our benefit as individuals, nor are they meant to draw attention to ourselves. Too often spiritual gifts are highlighted by the individuals who claim to have them. We all have images of those who make a profit off of their miraculous activities on television. But the truth is the same for everyone in the body of Christ; the Holy Spirit gifts those whom He wills for the purposes determined by God. No one owns their gift, the Holy Spirit does. *God* works within us so that others in the body will be edified, lifted up, encouraged, healed and exhorted. The power belongs to Him as we are mere vessels used as He directs us to perform the work of the ministry.

The attention is never to be directed at the person with the gift(s). The glory goes to the Lord. Sometimes we may wonder why certain people have been given certain gifts (like pastors and teachers), but we need to understand that the distribution of the gifts is God given. God sees His finished work in each of us, while we see the shortcomings of those who have been given certain gifts. We are not called to judge the person but to discern the work and to ensure Who is getting the glory. The Holy Spirit never brings attention to Himself, so His work within us is to be in the same manner. All credit in praise and thanksgiving belongs to the Lord. We are to be humble servants, used as the Lord wills and content to stay in the background. John the Baptist prayed as we should pray: "He must increase, but I must decrease." (John 3:30).

As we begin this lesson, our prayers should also reflect hearts that are willing to ask to be used as His vessels so that others will be blessed. It is an unselfish, loving and humble position to place yourself in, but it is essential for the fulfillment of the Holy Spirit's purposes.

This lesson will look at the spiritual gifts as discussed in the scriptures, why we receive them, how we should use them, can we lose them, and other points on this topic. Before we get started, let's pray:

Dear Lord, I ask that You prepare my heart and mind as we study about gifts and callings. Help me to remain focused and committed to studying Your word and praying for Your Holy Spirit to teach me how to apply the scriptures to my life. I pray that this lesson will open my eyes to all that You have for me in the area of spiritual gifts. May I truly be Your servant, humble and useful to performing the work of the ministry as You lead me. Let this be a time of joy and encouragement for Your body as we seek Your face together. In Jesus name, Amen.

Lesson 4: Gifts and Callings

Read Romans 12, 1 Corinthians 12 & 13, Ephesians 4

The Holy Spirit is responsible for giving us the gifts necessary to perform the work of the ministry. The Holy Spirit empowers us for testimony and service. The gifts of the Spirit are varied and diverse which pose much discussion as to how we receive them, how we use them, and can we lose them. One main point to remember is that the gifts are used for the body of Christ. The gifts are not to bring attention to ourselves but to bring glory to God. The Lord calls us for His purposes and equips us as He wills. Sometimes we may wonder why certain people have been given certain gifts (like pastors and teachers), but we need to understand that the distribution of the gifts is God given. We are not called to judge such things, but to support the work of the ministry. It is through the Holy Spirit that these gifts and callings are used in us and through us. Those of us who have been given certain gifts must develop the character to handle them appropriately. God is responsible for helping us mature in His ways: we are each His workmanship. He is more than able to accomplish the things that concern Him and His church.

Ephesians for gifts

Question 1: To better understand our position in terms of "works," briefly summarize the main point of the verses below.

a. Galatians 2:16

Not justify by works.

b. Ephesians 2:8-9

By grace not works

c. Ephesians 2:10: Who are we?

d. Ephesians 2:10: What were we created for?

to do good work

We are God's workmanship created to do His good works. Gifts are given to us to perform the "works" for the body of Christ, manifested with the fruits. They are not of us or from us, they are from God to be used for His purposes. We can receive His gifts and calling at any time. Gifts are not taken away, they are irrevocable (Romans 11:29). Some will become dormant as other gifts are needed to be stronger throughout different seasons of life. Only Jesus could walk in the fullness of the Spirit, using all the gifts because the Spirit was given to Him without limit (John 3:34). There is a difference between innate gifts and spiritual gifts. Natural gifts, skills and talents are different from supernatural gifts because we are born with them. We often confuse our natural gifts with those the Holy Spirit gives us. There are clear differences, especially in how they are used and who is in control of them.

Question 2: Before discussing the different spiritual gifts in the New Testament, answer the following questions as to what you have (or think you have) today.

a. List some of your natural gifts. How long have you known you had them?

Evangelize – since got save

b. List your spiritual gifts. How long have you had them?

Evangelize

c. How do you know if you have spiritual gifts? What confirmation do you have that you have been given a spiritual gift?

To receive a spiritual gift means that something is different about us. We have an ability that we never had before. The change is usually obvious because it is not of us, and it is not learned or earned; it is a gift. However, there are natural gifts that we have had our whole lives and have used for our own purposes that God can also use for His purposes. These gifts are not necessarily used for spiritual purposes because they are innate. But when a person surrenders his or her life over to the will of God, then the Lord takes ownership of that natural gift. The Holy Spirit will begin to work through us using those gifts as well as the ones He will supernaturally give us. For example, suppose someone is musically gifted and develop these artistic abilities and talents. That person can use that gift in many ways in the world, possibly even earn a living with it. But when that person comes to Christ, the Holy Spirit dwells in that person and wants to use that gift for the purposes of God. When the gift is surrendered to the Holy Spirit's control, there is a change that must take place as ownership is transferred from the person to the

Lord. This change is difficult for us in our flesh. We are so used to doing things in our flesh, under our own authority and choices, that to relinquish control of it can be very challenging. Our thoughts and behaviors must be retrained in the Lord. We must be willing to die to self, to decrease, so that the Lord will take over and use every part of us for His will. God does not use us because of our skills; He uses us because of our willingness to surrender to Him. Many people cannot make the transition between using their gifts and talents for personal use to surrendering to the Lord for the benefit of the church. God's ways are not our ways. We cannot think that what was success in the world will work in the church.

The first thing that God usually addresses is the pride that is associated with the "successful" individual. We are a body, not individuals in the ministry. God does not need any of us. We have to remember that God is not in a rush. If He wants something to succeed, it will be in His timing and in His ways. Self control is also a fruit of the Spirit that has to be learned when working in the gifts of the Spirit. It is to our pleasure to be used for His works.

Question 3: **Why are we given spiritual gifts? List the reasons in Ephesians 4:12-13.**

a. to equip

b. build up body of Christ

c. knowledge

Question 4: Look up the following verses and list the spiritual gifts as given.

a. Romans 12:6-8

Prophesy

b. 1 Corinthians 12:8-10

c. 1 Corinthians 12:28-30

d. Ephesians 4:11

Spiritual gifts are distributed by the Holy Spirit as He chooses. "*But one and the same Spirit works all these things, distributing to each one individually as He wills.*" *(1 Corinthians 12:11)* Paul compares the gifts of the Spirit to the members of our bodies. Each member has a function that is necessary for the health of the whole body. Eyes give sight, ears are for hearing, legs are for walking, lungs give us the ability to breathe, and even our big toe is necessary for balance.

Removing one piece would hinder the function of the whole body. Spiritual gifts are distributed to the members of the body of Christ for the same purpose…to ensure that the body functions as a whole, healthy unit. If one member suffers, then the whole body suffers. If one member rejoices, then the whole body rejoices.

The gifts listed in Ephesians 4 are given with other gifts. If you are a gifted teacher, you will need wisdom in handling the scriptures. If you are a pastor, you should have aspects of evangelism. We each can receive more than one gift. Jesus tells us in Luke 11:13 to ask for more of the Holy Spirit. And remember the Spirit is not limited; He will give us whatever gift we need if we are willing to serve the body or testify about Jesus.

Love
calvary
Calvin = / Presbeterian
T - total depravity
U - unlimited
L - limited atonement
I - Irrestable grace
P -

Wesley = focus on the love
metodist
nazarene

Question 5: How have you personally witnessed the use of spiritual gifts in the body of Christ?

Spiritual gifts generally fall into two categories: service/equipping and sign/testimony. The majority of the gifts are used in the service and work of the ministry, but certain gifts are given just to validate God's message as sent through His messenger. Gifts of service include administration, hospitality, serving, giving, leading and mercy. Gifts of signs and testimony include words of knowledge, prophecy, and tongues/interpretation of tongues.

Question 6: We need to actively ask for gifts. The Bible teaches us to ask and to pray for them. What do the following verses tell us to ask and seek after?

a. 1 Kings 3:9 (What did Solomon ask of the Lord?)

wisdom

b. Proverbs 2:2-3

understanding

c. Luke 11:13

more holy

d. 1 Corinthians 14:1

phopecy things

e. Ephesians 3:19

w

f. James 1:5

wisdom

The Holy Spirit moves actively within us and through us, using the gifts in the same kind of manner. Our gifts flow freely and are used conjunctively together. They are not independent of each other. We pray for more and we keep asking for the Spirit's continual filling of His gifts. Wisdom, knowledge and understanding, for example, are foundational to using the gifts for the body of Christ. We need to ask for these things without ceasing. We are not to get too focused on just one gift. The Lord will use many gifts at different times for different purposes. But we must be in a conscious state of prayer to keep asking, seeking and knocking so that we may receive and apply them as He directs us. And remember, the Lord will use us in situations regardless of a specific gifting, just ask Him. Ask the Lord to help you witness to someone and whether or not you have the gift of evangelism, God will give you the ability to do it as long as you are willing.

Question 7: What spiritual gifts do you believe the Lord has placed in your heart to earnestly seek?

✓ encouragging

wisdom
knowledge } gifts to ask the Lord
disturment

Phofecy = speaking the mind of God thraught the Spirit

Question 8: What happens to our gifts if we have setbacks or diversions in our Christian walk?

a. How did we get them? See Titus 3:5.

b. Can we lose God's gifts? See Romans 11:29.

c. What do you think happens to the gifts if we walk in disobedience against the Lord?

The Bible tells us that God's gifts and callings are irrevocable and it is by His mercy that we have anything at all. As long as we are walking with the Lord, heeding His voice, and applying His word to our lives, then we will continue to mature in the use of His gifts. But, if we choose to turn from the Lord, seek after our own desires, and rebel against His guidance, then we will not be sensitive to His workings within us. We are not focused on others if we are focused on ourselves, so the use of the gifts decrease and lie dormant until we return to the Lord.

Question 9: How do we begin to apply what we have learned to our lives? The first step is to ***step out***.

a. Mark 9:23

b. Matthew 21:22

c. John 15:16

To apply what we have learned, we must believe. We must believe that God's word is true. We must believe that the Holy Spirit is working within us. We must believe that the gifts given to us are real and functional. We must be willing to step out in faith and exercise the gifts, trusting in the Lord's purposes for them. We cannot act on feelings or emotions, but on faith. We must pray and seek the Lord's will in all things. We must continually ask for more of His Spirit, to pray without ceasing and to persevere in those prayers. We must be willing to surrender our control to His authority in all areas of our lives, including those natural gifts that we have relied upon in the past. If we are willing to submit to God's will, then whatever we ask in prayer, believing in faith, will be received.

Question 10: As a final petition of this study, write your own prayer asking the Lord to anoint you with the gifts He desires to give you. Use scripture verses to pray back to the Lord and keep this prayer in your heart as you ask, seek and knock for more of His Holy Spirit to fill you to overflowing.

Final thoughts:

"Most assuredly, I say to you, a servant is not greater than his master; nor is he who is sent greater than he who sent him." **John 13:16**

We need to remember that we are the Lord's servants, gifted to do His work. We do not tell God what needs to be done, He tells us. Pray that the desires of your heart are the ones that the Lord has placed there. Pray those desires back to Him, asking Him to use you to accomplish those tasks. If He has truly told you something to pray for, then He is responsible to achieve that goal. Do not worry and do not rush. He has a plan and He is able. Stay focused, stay committed to Him and stay in prayer. We are just servants that have become friends of our Master and Lord. Like Jesus says in **Matthew 5:16** "*Let your light so shine before men, that they may see your good works and glorify your Father in heaven.*" The Glory goes to God because of the love of Jesus.

From our hearts to yours....

As the participant of this study, our prayer for you was founded in Acts 4:31:

After they prayed, the place where they were meeting was shaken. And they were all filled with the Holy Spirit and spoke the word of God boldly.

We all want a prayer life that shakes the foundations of our lives. We want to live in the power and presence of the Lord every day. We want to be filled with the Holy Spirit to speak the word of God boldly and to be used in His service. We hope that these desires were shared by you as they were the desires of our hearts in writing this study. We also pray that you have personally seen the Lord move in your heart to better understand the heart of God for all of us.

The Lord loves us so much that He gave His only begotten Son to die for our sins so that we may be saved. Jesus left heaven to come to earth for us. Our heavenly Father had a plan from the beginning and that plan is one of redemption. God desired to redeem us back from the bondage of sin so He may dwell with His people on earth. Without Jesus and His death on the cross, our sins would forever separate us from God. God just wants to be with us; God wants to be with you personally. Hard to believe? But because of Jesus, we not only can come to the Father, but we can have His Spirit dwelling within us. We believe, so we can receive.

However, as Christians, we still deal with the things that try and tempt us to fail. We still must deal with the enemy who will use every tactic possible to hinder our walk and our work. We also fight against our own desires of the flesh. Lastly, we fight against the pattern of the world, attempting to allure us to its ways. This is why it is so important that we know the truth. The truth is that we have been given God's Spirit; we are sealed with His guarantee for eternity and are empowered to do the things He calls us to do. Many Christians today live defeated lives, not knowing how to break the snare that entangles them. The answer lies in knowing how to live in the Spirit.

How, then, can we live a Spirit-filled life that God wants each of us to have? In review, we must believe, we must pray and ask for Him to give us evidence of His fruits in our lives. We need to ask Him for gifts for the edification of the body of believers and to witness and do His service. We must surrender everything to Him. We cannot live a Spirit-filled life outside of God's will. We will know the truth of His word when we are reading and meditating on it daily. We will know the fullness of His grace and mercy when we personally know the One who tells us to claim those things with boldness. We will understand the Lord's teachings when we ask His Holy Spirit to open our minds and hearts. We will bear good fruit and be given His gifts when we submit to His control and authority in our lives. Evidence of a Spiritb filled life is a changed life, being transformed from glory to glory as we are conformed into the image of Christ.

The victory comes when we surrender to the truth of His words and when we are being led by the Spirit. We must decrease and Jesus must increase. When we truly take our eyes off of ourselves and put our complete focus on Jesus, then we will see the Holy Spirit take control. We will see "rivers of living water" flow from our hearts because we thirst for Jesus. (John 7:38) Our lives will bear witness of Him and will bring glory and honor to His holy name. Life in the Spirit is the only life that matters because it starts here and counts unto eternity.

As we close out this study on "Life in the Spirit," we want to give thanks to the Lord for His faithfulness to see us through to completion. We serve an awesome God who has given us His Holy Spirit to indwell our hearts and lives. We pray that you have personally seen the workings of the Holy Spirit in your life during these past few weeks. We pray that you have a hunger and thirst for more of Him, in confidence knowing that He is always with you, wanting to work in and through you. May God reign in your life today.

Bobbye Brooks & Tonilee Adamson Email: info@dailydisciples.org

For more information, visit us at www.dailydisciples.org or call 1-800-992-0369.

Calling

Gifts = Work = fruit = faithful Joy

earth — eternal

+ Love

prayer

Matthew 25:14

talents — time

platform

job fam. town

5

2 2

1 =

double it

Pray to evangelize the

on the hunger of the

words

50152790R00045

Made in the USA
Charleston, SC
15 December 2015